It has been told that the ancient yogis in India had discovered the secret to ultra-longevity, vitality, and virility.

And what is that secret?

It is the mastery of sacred sexual energy for the joy, bliss, vitality, and continual rejuvenation of the body, the path to immortality.
Are you interested in sacred sex?
It' s total bliss beyond your wildest dreams.

Join me in a life-changing discussion.

About the Author

Cfayla Johnson is a natural healer whose focus is spiritual energetic rejuvenation. Upon her awakening in September 2011, she felt such overwhelming, unconditional love and gratitude, she was moved to share her knowledge, so all may join her in living a life fueled by love energy and bliss. Cfayla lives in the Miami, Florida, area where she moved to write the second and third book in her trilogy, Be Enlightened Now.

Sacred Sexuality and Immortality in the Age of Enlightenment:

Divine Cosmic Energy as the Path to Blissful Immortality

Book Two in the Trilogy "Be Enlightened Now"

AND
Beach Foodie Goes Global

Expanding the Divine Enlightenment of Food

Book Three in the Trilogy "Be Enlightened Now"

By Cfayla Johnson

BALBOA.
PRESS
A DIVISION OF HAY HOUSE

Copyright © 2012 Cfayla Johnson

ISBN: 978-1-4525-6054-0 (sc)
ISBN: 978-1-4525-6055-7 (e)

Library of Congress Control Number: 2012919484

Balboa Press books may be ordered through booksellers or by contacting:

Balboa Press
A Division of Hay House
1663 Liberty Drive
Bloomington, IN 47403
www.balboapress.com
1-(877) 407-4847

Printed in the United States of America

Balboa Press rev. date: 10/17/2012

Thank you to Cliff Roles and David Knaggs for the author photos.

Dedicated to my mentors, with eternal love and gratitude.

Very OLD SCHOOL is very NEW SCHOOL. It has been told that the ancient yogis in India had discovered the secret to ultra longevity, vitality, and virility. This secret was kept well hidden for thousands of years except to a few privalaged and highly trained masters. And what is that secret?

The SECRET is the mastery of sacred sexual energy for the joy, bliss, vitality, and continual rejuvenation of the physical body, the creativity and realization of your most desired dreams, and the feeling of unconditional love this energy brings to every cell of your body. This energy is limitless, knows no bounds, and is available to all. To live in this energy IS the state of ENLIGHTENMENT and is a LEARNABLE skill and PROCESS. Finally, would you like to know what it's like to live like this and how you can join in on the unconditional love, joy, and fun of the enlightened state?

Are you interested in sacred sex, it's total bliss beyond your wildest dreams, the power of creating and realizing your desires and regenerating your body?

If any of this sounds appealing, then I invite you to join me in one of the most provacative discussions we can have as human beings.

Love, love, love: for love is all there is....

Cfayla

Foreward:

This book is actually two books, the second and third book in the trilogy called

"Be Enlightened Now"

Book 1: Beach Foodie

Book 2: Sacred Sexuality and Immortality in the Age of Enlightenment

Book 3: Beach Foodie Goes Global

Books two and three are written to illustrate the concept of sacred male and female energy.

The "masculine" energy is depicted by book two being written in the traditional DECENDING

Style while book three is depicting the sacred "feminine" energy by being written back to front,

meeting book two in the middle of the publication where the two books meet in the energy

Of unconditional love. The "Do It" portion of "Beach Foodie Goes Global" is also written

From the bottom to the top of the page, as sacred "feminine" energy rises in an upward

ASCENT within the energetic centers of the body. The reading of these two books is a

Recipe for experiencing the flow of male and feminine energy, and is meant to celebrate

The beauty and merging of both energies in the age of enlightenment. The book has two

Covers: the front cover is for book two, "masculine" energy and the back cover is for book

Three, "feminine" energy; each cover honoring the sacred divinity of both energies.

This book is written so that the reader must focus and be aware of how to read the book.

Both of these qualities are needed to go inward and begin the process of mastering the

Divine spiritual energy which resides in you. Reading the book will give you practice in staying

Focused and in the "present" moment.

I have already joined you as "one " by writing the book in this way. The writing challenged me

to CREATE, FOCUS, with AWARENESS, and LOVE. You are GREATLY loved.

Table of Contents

Sacred Sexual Energy Basics:

SACRED SEXUAL energy is divine energy coming from the SOURCE of all creation, the source of unconditional love in our cosmos. LOVE energy is the most powerful energy available to us. This ENERGY has a MASCULINE energy which is ACTIVE in nature and a FEMININE energy which is RECEPTIVE in nature. Both are equally POWERFUL and exist in each of us. These energies FLOW within our bodies; controlling our breath, our automatic body functions every moment of our lives. To CONSCIOUSLY and with AWARENESS access this energy, brings us great power to TRANFORM our lives, our relationships, our VERY existence.

ENERGETIC CENTERS of the body are gateways to the flow of ENERGY in our body; both feminine and masculine. When these energetic centers are free from obtacles blocking the FLOW of energy, profound changes occur in the regeneration of the body. The SACRED SEXUAL energy FLOWS from the base of the spine, upward through the ENERGY centers in a channel that goes from the spine to the TOP of the HEAD. The SEXUAL FEMININE energy uncoils as it releases and moves upward to join the MASCULINE energy at the TOP of the HEAD. This movement of ENERGY FEELS LIKE a BEAM of LIGHT moving within your BODY.

1

ONCE the ENERGIES join and MERGE together, the ENERGY of the DIVINE ENERGY of the COSMOS is perfectly balanced in UNION. They MEET at the HEART energy CENTER, now in the ENERGY of unconditional love of the DIVINE. When these ENERGIES are MERGED and moving from the HEART center, they HEAL the body, and regenerate the CELL. The energy is so powerful, it removes blockages in the energy of the body, physical, emotional, spiritual, to INCREASE the FLOW, revitalizing us, giving us great VIRILITY and YOUTH.

WHEN the MERGED energy reaches a STRONG enough FORCE, IT changes the STRUCTURE of the CELLS of the body in a POWERFUL, explosion of ENERGY. This is an AWAKENING of ENERGY and permanently changes the ABILITY of the BODY, making it a SUPERCONDUCTOR of DIVINE SEXUAL energy for a life of LOVE, BLISS, HEALTH, and the fullfillment of YOUR dreams.

As this ENERGY is moved FREQUENTLY, at some point, it may no longer be CONFINED to moving WITHIN the energy centers of the body and may FREEFLOW throughout the ENTIRE body. WHEN this occurs, THE ENERGY Center of the TOP of the HEAD is released, making it open to become a MAGNET and MASSIVE channel for RECEIVING of DIVINE energy.

WHEN a couple engages in SACRED SEXUALITY when both of them are in a state of balanced ENERGY within their own bodies, the COMBINED SEXUAL ENERGY of the COUPLE gives them great feelings of UNCONDITIONAL LOVE for each other, EXPANDS the ORGASMIC experience to the FULL BODY which LASTS for several minutes or HOURS, and REBUILDS and VITALIZES the CELLS as the ENERGY that is normally lost during SEX, is CONTAINED in the BODY and CIRCULATED within the BODY to HEAL, to REGENERATE, TO PROVIDE BLISS.

This BLISS state is the STATE of ENLIGHENMENT, from WHERE you CAN MANIFEST your DEEPEST desires. THE POWER of the SEXUAL ORGASM from this ENERGY is INFINITELY STRONGER than a NONDIVINE Sexual experience.

LIVING the BLISS is MOVING this ENERGY within your body and as a COUPLE daily. First you balance the FEMININE and MASCULINE energies within yourself, ALLOW the FREE flow of ENERGY to move within YOU, then you may COMBINE your balanced energy with your PARTNER as you ENHANCE your SEXUAL EXPERIENCE.

IMMORTALITY comes when you are able to move the SACRED Sexual ENERGY so POWERFULLY and FREQUENTLY that it REMOVES all OBSTACLES to the PERFECT HEALTH of the CELL, thereby making IMMORTALITY and the ENLIGHTENED state, the NEW NORMAL for your body

ENERGY CENTERS LOCATION	FUNCTION	COLOR
ROOT Base of Spine	Survival and Grounding	RED
SACRAL Tailbone	Desire, Sexuality, Creativity	ORANGE
SOLAR PLEXIS Diaphram	Will and Power	YELLOW
HEART Heart	Love and Compassion	GREEN/PINK
THROAT Throat	Communication	BLUE
3rd EYE Between the EYES	Intuition, Imagination, Wisdom	INDIGO
CROWN Top of the HEAD	Spirituality, Understanding	VIOLET

Recipes for Moving Energy: Energy FOLLOWS Awareness

Sunshine Centering:

This recipe provides a way to become aware of the energy centers in your body starting with your heart. The heart connects the lower and upper energy centers, thus this technique is called "centering". You may do this exercise several times a day when you desire a feeling for calmness, joy, and love.

Ingredients:

Quiet Mind: Take a few moments in this exercise to clear your mind of all thought except to focus your attention on your heart

Breath: Begin to take long deep, breaths, bringing your attention to your heart.

Focus and Awareness: Continue to focus on your heart and imagine the sun entering your heart and expanding golden sunshine into your heart. Continue to breath deeply and focus on expanding the sunshine outward in your heart including the back of your heart. Take at least 7 deep breaths and continue to bring the sunshine into your heart.

Rainbow Making:

In this recipe, we begin to focus energy and awareness into each of our seven major energy centers. This technique allows you to begin to be aware of and feel energy in each energy center. It also allows for the beginning of removing obstacles to the flow of energy in the energy center. If you become distracted at any time, say "thank you" and refocus on the energy center and color of the rainbow where you left off. You may also go back to your heart center at any time and focus on sunshine centering.

Quiet Mind

Breath

Focus and Awareness

To begin, start with the sunshine centering exercise to quiet your mind and center on your energy centers.

You will then focus on each energy center, beginning with the top of the head and moving downward. For each energy center, you will focus on the energy center and imagine the color of that energy center expanding into that space. Take at least seven deep breaths, continuing to focus on the color of the energy center before moving to the next energy center.

You will be making an energy rainbow which you will create starting at the top of your head and ending at the base of your spine. It will have the following colors in this order:

Violet- top of the head

Indigo- between the eyes

Blue- Throat

Green- Heart

Yellow- Diaphram

Orange- Tailbone

Red- Base of Spine

Once you have made your rainbow, you will have taken 49 deep breaths and focused awareness of each of your energy centers. By visualizing and bringing light and color to your energy centers, you bring energy to it, and begin to remove obstacles to the flow of energy within your body. You are in the beginning stages of accessing the divine energy of the cosmos.

Practice at least twice a day, preferably at sunrise and sunset. You may begin to add meditative music and spend more time focusing on each energetic center as you build your rainbow.

Beam of Light:

In this recipe, we are going to begin moving energy within the body through the seven energy centers. This will feel like a beam of light is moving through your body.

Begin with sunshine centering, and make your rainbow with your energy centers. Your rainbow will have ended at the base of the spine with a focus on the color red.

Quiet mind

Breath

Focus/Awareness

As you focus on your root energy center at the base of your spine, imagine a column, a cylinder which runs from the base of your spine to the top of your head. This column is the divine energy channel within your body. You may not feel it at first, just imagine that it exists. As you continue to breath, slowly change the red color at the base of your spine to a golden light. You may imagine a golden ball of light. Begin to move this light upwards to your next energy center as if it were a beam of light. Continue to move it upward in your energy channel through each of your energy centers until you reach the top of your head. You may then move the beam of light downward in your energy channel, through the energy centers back down to the base of the spine.

Once you start to feel the sensation of a light beam moving through your energy centers, you may do "sunshine centering" at any time and then move directly to "Beam of Light". This recipe bringing vitality and vigor to your energy centers, clearing them of stress and bringing vigor and vitality to those areas of the body. You are beginning to feel the movement of divine spiritual energy within your body.

As you begin to move the energy, you may say "thank you" repeatedly as a mantra. Gratitude is a high energy and will assist in the flow of energy within your body.

Swirling and Twirling:

In this recipe, we are going to make our rainbow, and as we make the rainbow, we are going to move energy within each energy center, to assist in removing any obstacles to the flow of energy. This is swirling the energy.

Quiet Mind

Breath

Focus and Awareness

As you begin to build your rainbow starting with violet at the top of your head, imagine you are expanding the color violet into the top of your head and begin gently swirling the energy in a clockwise motion, making little circles of violet. After seven breaths, reverse the swirling of the violet color to counterclockwise. Then imagine the energy swirling out the back of your head, taking with it anything you would like to dissolve with it, headache, stress, tension, etc.

Move through each energy center in turn and swirl the energy, then swirl it out the back of each energy center, taking anything that no longer serves you with the energy leaving your body. You may also imagine you are swirling and twirling love energy into your energy centers as you build your rainbow.

At any time, you may focus on one energy center if there is something specific you would like to bring into your life. If you want more love and compassion, swirl energy into your heart center, then swirl out of the back of your heart anything that no longer serves you.

Practice several times a day, especially in the evening before you go to bed. Over time, this helps to remove obstacles to the flow of energy in your body. Continue to breath throughout the exercise as breath is the conductor of the energy.

Looping for Love:

Looping energy moves energy through the energetic centers in a systematic loop type movement. Looping of energy through the energy centers greatly increases the movement of energy. Along with breathing as you loop the energy, this powerful practice ignites the female and male energies of the body, allowing the flow of energy to reach a tipping point, where the energy is strong enough to "ignite" the cells to change their structure.

Begin by "centering" your energy. This exercise is similiar to beam of light except energy is beamed to specific energy centers in a loop to assist in balancing and merging the male and female energy of the body.

Once you have centered in your heart, focus on your root energy center.

Then move your focus to the top of your head, focusing on the top of your head.

Move back down to the root and focus your awareness, then move your focus up to the

The energy center between your eyes.

Move back down to the root, focus your awareness, then move your focus to the energy center in your throat.

Return to the root and continue to loop the energy through each of the remaining energy centers until you have arrived back at the root.

This looping greatly helps in moving the male energies downward and the female energy upwards to balance and merge the male and female energy.

Once you are at the root, then move the focus to the heart center.

Then move the energy to the tailbone and focus the energy on the sacral energy center.

Return to the heart center and focus the energy to the heart center.

Then move the energy to the diaphram and focus on the solar plexis energy center.

Keep returning to the heart center as you loop the energy upwards into each energetic center finishing with the top of the head.

Now return to the root, focus the energy, then move the energy to the top of the head and imagine a loop of light energy moving from the base of the spine to the top of the head in an energy loop, moving through each of the energy centers as the loop continues. You may move the looping energy faster and continue to breath through each loop.

This is an excellent exercise for couples to practice together, each looping their own energy and synchronizing their breathing in preparation for the looping of energy as a couple during sacred sex.

Grounding:

This recipe is used after every energy movement exercise. After you have completed the exercise, even if it is short, imagine the energy you created moving through your legs and grounding you to the earth. Imagine roots going down into the earth, anchoring you to the power of the earth.

This is important for bringing the energy into your physical world and allowing you to use the energy for life on earth. It brings you back in touch with your physical surroundings.

Protective Shield

This recipe empowers you to surround yourself with divine spiritual energy to protect your

energy to preserve and protect you.

Quiet Mind

Focus

Awareness

At any time, you may protect your divine energy by quieting your mind, and imagining a golden

Shield, Veil, or Cloak surrounding your body with divine energy and light. Imagine only good

Divine energy and experience will be allow to come to you and you will be protected from all

Negativity. Imagine the negative bouncing off you while all good comes to you with ease and

Grace. Express your gratitude for this protection to the universe.

ENLIGHTENMENT MODEL:
Staying in the FLOW

To be in an ENLIGHTENED state, is to be energetically connected with the divine energy of the cosmos each moment. To stay in the FLOW and access this limitless energy, there are four parts to the model.

QUIET MIND: The more you can quiet the mind and consciously and with awareness connect with the divine energy of the cosmos and MOVE that energy, the more ENLIGHTENED you will become. This is a process which requires patience and focus. If your mind feels busy, say "thank you", until your mind can become quiet.

BREATH: Your breath is your connection to the divine. As you practice deep breathing during these energy moving techniques, you are connecting to the energy from the cosmos which keeps your body working without your thought. By focusing on your BREATH, you are focusing with awareness on connecting with the most powerful energy that exists, PURE LOVE ENERGY.

FOCUS and AWARENESS: Your focus and awareness moving INWARD, connects you to the vast energy available within your body. FEMININE energy resides INWARD and allowing this energy to MOVE and merge with the MASCULINE energy from the DIVINE, brings you perfect balance and the ability to transform your life.

LOVE and GRATITUDE: Continual thoughts of love and gratitude for every aspect of your life will free you and bring you more of your hearts DEEPEST DESIRES and greater ability to tap into the energy of the cosmos. Each time you express love and say thank you, you are connecting with the divine sacred love energy, the most powerful ENERGY of the cosmos.

Do It! A Story of Enlightened Sacred Sex

Sedona Swadhishtana took a deep breath. She began to focus inward on her breath, quieting

her mind, relaxing it as she began to sway to the beating of the drums and the sounds of the

guitar, as her beloved, Mooladhara, strummed the guitar for her. A simple sound, the chords he

was playing, as he gazed upon her with loving eyes. She loved the fire ceremonies of the full

and new moon, especially sharing them with Mooli. The fire was huge, built in a massive free

standing fire place, enticing, building the love and compassion of all who gazed upon it. It was

especially powerful on the full moon.

As Sedona began her swaying she moved closer to Mooli. She began to visualize a golden

light at the base of her spine, expanding and beginning to allow her divine feminine energy to

begin it's slow dance in her body, beginning it's upward ascent through her energy channel and energy centers. Already the energy was feeling delicious, tingling, shimmering as it began to

unfold. As she focused her awareness, her eyes connected with Mooli's, and she began to

imagine golden light extending from her eyes to his eyes, in greeting and in love. This beautiful

love energy connection began to build a sacred sexual energy, a fire, in her and in Mooli at the

same time. Almost without thought, she moved the golden light to the base of her pubic

bone, expanding the color into a beautiful soft orange, flooding her energy into this sacred

center. She could feel the energy release as it built and expanded upward, the intensity, the

heat, the desire build in her. Mooli's eyes were upon her, focusing his awareness and energy on

the same area in his body, and sending her an energetic beam at the same time. Anticipation

was in his eyes, deep unconditional love for Sedona and they moved closer to each other. They

were so close they were almost touching, it felt like deep, loving caresses flowing back and forth

between them. They began to dance around each other, as they moved around the sacred fire,

eyes locked in sacred embrace and love. They began to move their awareness to the diaphram,

their power centers expanding with golden yellow light and the energy continued to build.

There started to be an element of letting go totally for both of them, riding the energy they

were creating. Now the sacred energy of the feminine became stronger in both of them as they

began to be filled with sexual desire, so primal, so deep, it was exquisite. The energy builds,

their breathing now becoming much more focused, as they started to sychronize their breath,

building the energy, pushing away and releasing any obstacles to deep unconditional love.

Sedona's cells started to sing and vibrate, and she could feel a tightness of desire building in her

in anticipation of their divine merging, physically and energetically. Now Mooli and Sedona

moved the energy to their heart, bursting forth with a sparkling shower of love and they

carressed the energy and allowed it to move to expand first their own heart, then to each

other's heart, as they made an ancient deep connection with their souls. Their energy expanded

outward, close to each other, yet not quite merged. They began to touch and Mooli began to

kiss Sedona, and touching her gently, allowing her to relax, surrender into the blissful energy of

the cosmos they were both beginning to feel. As they continued to build the energy, Sedona

began to moan softly, Mooli began kissing her more deeply. Now dancing together, touching, enjoying the energy, Mooli began moving them both toward a beautiful cabana, tucked in near

the gorgeous waterfall; the water rushing down the side of the hill, almost as if it were moving

straight into the fire, with the beautiful starlight surrounding them. They swayed and danced

into the cabana, now touching each other more deeply, making the energy stronger. As they

moved toward the hand carved wooden bed, they began to undress each other and move their

focus upward to their throats, into the upper energy centers. Mooli and Sedona began swirling

the energy through their throats, expanding it as broad as the sky. Mooli reached for Sedona

and removed her dress, pulling her on top of him in a playful motion. Quickly, she removed his

tunic and she playfully began to stroke his body. They kissed, touched, body to body, the

energy now beginning to merge. They began to move with each other and Sedona merged

Mooli inside her as they now began their joint rhythmic ascent to the third eye energy center.

Explosion of light, of flooding energy began to fill their bodies and they focused on this spiritual

eye, sending energy to each other, sexual, yes, and divine, loving, the energy of the cosmos now

being so close to them. Quicker and faster they moved, the energy now focusing on the top of their heads, the crown, filling the lotus with light. Moving, they reached the critical peak,

simultaneously, expanding and exploding into an orgasm so strong, so deep, they both cried out

in love and estacsy. The merging of the sacred feminine and sacred masculine was completed,

balanced in exqusite harmony. They could feel the energy of the orgasm flooding their bodies.

As they continued to focus on their crown energy center, Sedona began moving the energy

from her crown over to Mooli's crown, looping down through his energy centers. Then she

moved the energy over to her root energy center, allowing the orgasm to rise and loop upward

to her crown, and continuing to loop the energy of her orgasm through both of them. She kept

her focus on the crown, on her spiritual energy center, combining the sacred divine energy with

the energy of her orgasm. The shaking and quivering of her own body in it's orgasmic bliss,

added to the intensity. The orgasm continued strong, pulsing massive energy into each cell of

Sedona and Mooli's bodies. There was no control for Sedona, wild life force energy exploded

through her and she rode the energy like a giant wave. At the same time, Mooli began looping

his orgasmic energy through his energy centers, joining her in this magical orgasmic energy loop,

A protective cloak around their bodies to preserve this divine energy.

End of Book Two

Beginning of the book:

Global Goes Foodie Beach:

Johnson Cfayla by

.ONE as FIRST the join shall LAST The

!you of all to love, love, Love

Cfayla

Johnson Zack :to Dedicated

This fabulous planet

Enlightenment right now, and you can be/ and ARE a part of it by being on

Living in the age of

Is written, and the energetic message it sends. We are all ONE, we are

The way the book

Beach Foodie Goes Global is a celebration of sacred "feminine" energy in

Visited.

Simple, high life force beach foodie recipies, inspired by the locations I

Miami. They are

Of my travels including Costa Rica, the Florida Keys, Ft Lauderdale, and

great recipes from all

Hi everyone! I'm back again with another two books! I have another 30

Table of Contents:

Beach Foodie Global Recipes:

We are now leaving Siesta Key Beach in Florida where "Beach Foodie" was written and

taking a global foodie journey to Costa Rica, the Florida keys, and the global city of Miami, and

the beautiful beaches of southern Florida on the Atlantic side.

The food and recipes reflect the adventure and spirit of people, the food available, and

The uniquely inspired recipies each place gave to me. This is just the beginning as I begin

To work my way around the globe; bringing new Beach foodie recipies to the planet. Stayed

tuned, I want to pair my food with the world's best wines in

"Divine Pairings"

Light Beam to You!

Pacific Yoga Board Grateful Greens Soup :

Organic spinach and arugala

Cold pressed olive oil

Mix together.

Raw sunflower seeds

Raw pecans

Sprinkle on top of salad mixture.

Add organic salt and pepper.

Allow to chill.

Add fresh spring water to taste and garnish with chopped green olives or ginger if desired.

No cooking needed, this is a cold/room temperature soup.

A great way to stay hydrated, get high life force greens, and protein.

In honor of the fabulous Yogaboard on the Pacific Ocean.

Montana del Edyn Waterfall Egg Salad:

Flavored cold pressed olive oil (lemon or lime)

Costa Rican local raw, unheated, unfiltered honey

Cooked egg whites

Raw pumpkin seeds

Raw sunflower seeds

Mix together and enjoy. A great source of raw fat, protein, and honey for assimilation.

More fun when you have to cook the egg whites on an old fashioned, "match light" stove

With a "real" FLAME.

The combination of raw honey and olive oil makes a delightful raw dressing, providing you with

Energy and cleansing the body.

In honor of a Costa Rican paradise.

Pura Vida PB :

Costa Rican avocado, sliced-available at roadside stands all throughout the countryside

Fresh organic mushrooms, sliced

Green olives, diced.

Raw tahini to taste.

Raw sunflower seeds.

Mix and enjoy.

Great snack for before or after a

Standup paddleboard race in the Pacific Ocean AROUND an island and back.

Provides great energy for the long distance race.

Nosara Delight

Organic baby tomatoes, chopped

Raw tahini butter to taste

Raw walnuts, chopped.

3 green olives, chopped.

Cinammon.

Combine ingredients and enjoy as a quick snack.

In honor of the raw foods available in Nosara and great yoga and surfing in the area.

Energetic Spark Fruit Salad

Organic yellow grapefruit

Organic red cherries

Raw cocoanut butter

Raw unfiltered, unheated honey

3 pecans, chopped.

Combine ingredients. Provides an invigorating, low glycemic fruit combination and a great

Source of raw fat.

Tamarindo Costa Rican Seaweed Fantasy

Seaweed salad

Egg whites cooked in cocoanut oil

Raw sunflower seeds

Combine ingredients and enjoy!

A great blend of superfoods.

A tribute to the people of Tamarindo.

Langosta Costa Rican Sea Veggies Delight

Sea Veggies chopped and uncooked

Cold pressed olive oil to taste.

Spicy marinated veggies to taste.

Combine above three ingredients

Crunchy and tasty, great source of minerals.

A tribute to one of the world's treasures, the estuary.

Coral Gables Light Energy Delight

Heart of palm

Artichoke

Cold pressed olive oil

Raw vinegar

Raw walnuts

Red and orange peppers, diced.

Green olives, diced.

Provides a flavorable, highly nutritious salad to support the balancing of the male and

Female energies

5 Grandmothers Antipasto Salad

1 package sliced Vegan pepperoni

Red and yellow baby peppers, chopped

Green olives, diced

Marinated mushrooms

1 teaspoon flavored cold pressed olive oil.

Mix together for a high protein, raw fat combination

In honor of the Nicoya Penninsula in Costa Rica, where

People live to be very old with high life force energy. To their strong value

of family and to

honor the 5 five grandmothers.

Eggs and Bacon Stack:

Vegan canadian bacon cooked in cocoanut oil

Egg whites cooked in cocoanut oil

Green olives, diced

Avocado, sliced

1 teaspoon raw unheated, unfiltered, honey

Stack egg whites on top of Canadian bacon

Stack avocado on top of egg whites

Add green olives on top

Drizzle with raw honey if desired.

Buffed Up Burrito Stack:

Vegan canadian bacon cooked in cocoanut oil

Mexican Veggie "crumbles" cooked in cocoanut oil

Raw organic shreaded arugala

1 tablespoon cold pressed olive oil

Salt and pepper to taste

Combine oil and spices with greens.

Lay canadian bacon flat.

Stack crumbles on top of canadian bacon.

Add "greens" on top.

Add sliced avocado on top.

It's a hearty meal or snack, good protein, raw fat, and greens.

Fort Lauderdale Taco Salad:

Mexican veggies "crumbles" cooked in cocoanut oil

Add marinated giardiniera veggies on top.

Drizzle 1 tablespoon raw tahini on top.

1 tablespoon raw cocoanut butter.

Great source of protein and raw fat, veggies add crunch and spice.

Key Biscayne Canadian Wrap:

1 serving vegan candadian bacon cooked in cocoanut oil

Organic greens, sprouts, spinach, etc

1 teaspoon cold pressed olive oil

Salt and pepper to taste

Mix ingredients together for greens.

Use canadian bacon as the "wrap" with "greens" as the filling.

A healthy protein entre. Great source of protein, greens, and raw fat.

Brickell Chili:

1 package soy "Beef" crumbles cooked in cocoanut oil

One half large mushroom, sliced

Small amount of minced garlic

Diced green olives.

1 small organic onion, chopped.

1 teaspoon flavored cold pressed olive oil.

Add all ingredients uncooked to "beef" crumbles.

Add spring water with ingredients to soup like consistency AFTER cooking crumbles.

Organic salt and pepper to taste.

Great source of protein and raw fat.

In honor of Latin Dance in Brickell.

Nancy's Birthday Cake

Vanilla Sunwarrior Protein Powder

Raw cocoanut butter

Raw, unfilted, unheated, honey

Organic shreaded cocoanut

Raw cacao nibs

5 pecans, chopped

Small amount of vanilla almond milk

Mix together to the consistency of a "crumb" cake.

Highly nutritious cake, great source of raw fat and protein.

Put in a container and take to the tiki bar to celebrate a special birthday.

In honor of Nancy's birthday celebration.

Bridge Carmel Apple Stack:

Green apple coated in raw unheated, unfiltered honey

Then stack or drizzle 1 tablespoon raw cocoanut or almond butter over honey

Next stack raw pecans

Next stack organic shreaded cocoanut.

Next stack raw cacao nibs.

Chill.

Good source of raw protein and raw fat.

Dust with raw hemp seeds for more protein.

Leave off any ingredient you don't like, change it up! It's your Apple.

In honor of running the historic bridge near Marathon in the Florida Keys.

Boardwalk Vanilla Honey Float:

Raw pecans pieces (around 5)

1 tablespoon raw cocoanut butter

1 teaspoon raw, unfiltered, unheated honey

Vanilla almond milk.

Blend cocoanut mixture into a combination of vanilla milk and water.

A very good source of raw fat for energy and a great way to hydrate.

A great anytime snack.

South Beachy Reeces Peanut Butter Cup:

Raw almond butter.

1 teaspoon raw unfiltered, unheated honey

Mix together and spread out flat.

Raw cacao nibs.

Cover with cacao nibs.

Makes a crunchy, high protein, tasty snack.

Key Largo Almond Joy:

Raw cocoanut butter

Organic shreaded cocoanut.

1 teaspoon raw, unfiltered, unheated honey.

Raw almonds.

Combine above ingredients and cover in raw cacao nibs.

A nutritious alternative to an "Almond Joy" Enjoy!

Islamorada Key Lime Mash:

Lime juice

Organic shreaded cocoanut

1 teaspoon raw unheated, unfiltered honey

1 tablespoon cocoanut butter

1 teaspoon raw tahini butter

Raw sunflower seeds

Raw pumpkin seeds

Combine ingredients, tastes like key lime pie, great source of raw fat and protein.

In honor of the fabulous Greek tahini available near Islamorada.

Key West Raw Nut Brittle:

Raw cocoanut butter.

Raw tahini butter.

Raw walnuts.

1 teaspoon unheated, unfiltered, honey.

Any other raw nut of your choice.

Combine all ingredients, excellent source of raw fat, and protein.

Tahini gives it the "nut brittle" taste.

Spanish Candlelight Ice Cream:

1 tablespoon raw cocoanut cream.

1 teaspoon raw tahini butter.

1 teaspoon raw unheated, unfiltered, honey.

Organic raw walnuts, broken into pieces.

Small amount of vanilla almond milk.

Mix together and serve. An excellent source of raw fat and protein.

Freeze for ice cream consistency. Add raw hemp hearts for additional protein and crunch.

In honor of the language school in Tamarindo.

Brickell Yoga Cream and Ice Cream:

Small amount of vanilla almond milk

1 teaspoon raw unfiltered, unheated honey.

1 tablespoon raw cocoanut butter

Organic shreaded cocoanut, is desired.

Mix together and enjoy.

For "ice cream", freeze before eating.

A great light "ice cream", good source of raw fat and raw honey for assimilation.

In honor of the Brickell area of Miami, great snack after hot yoga.

4 Grandfathers Chocolate Covered Cherries:

Organic Cherries.

1 teaspoon raw, unheated, unfiltered honey

1 tablespoon raw, cocoanut butter

Raw cacoa nibs.

Mix honey and cocoanut together and cover the cherries in mixture.

Sprinkle raw cacoa nibs on top of cocoanut mixture.

In honor of Costa Ricans love of family and the 4 grandfathers.

Eye Candy Maple Fudge

1 packet raw walnut butter

1 teapoon organic maple butter

3 pecans, chopped

Mix together and enjoy. Good source of raw fat

Delicious!

Cocoanut La Dicha Bar

1 package raw cocoanut butter frozen

A half teaspoon of organic maple butter

3 raw pecans

Take frozen cocoanut butter out of package

Spread maple syrup on top

Stack pecans on top.

So delicious and easy! Individual packets of raw cocoanut butter are perfect for a single

Or double serving. Great source of raw fat.

Siesta Key Beach Enlightened Vanilla Latte

8 oz spring water

2 ounces vanilla almond milk

1 half teaspoon of organic maple butter

Heat spring water, then add vanilla almond milk.

Stir in maple syrup and enjoy.

Makes a nice drink in the evening before bed, a healthy latte.

Make it your own latte by adding less water, more almond milk.

In honor of where it all BEGAN.

Tango PB 2 Love Cup

PB2 peanut butter

Raw cocoanut butter

Raw unfiltered, unheated honey

Combine ingredients and chill.

Yummy and high in protein, providing a great source of raw fat.

In honor of the Tango in Miami

Tamarindo Cocoanut Water

1 large cocoanut

1 knife

friendly Costa Rican

Ask for cocoanut water. The top of the cocoanut will be cut off, a straw inserted, and the

Cocoanut handed back to you with a smile for you to drink the cocoanut water right out of the

Cocoanut.

Wonderfully refreshing!

Key West Popsicle:

Heavy plastic wine glass

Raw unheated, unfiltered honey

Raw cocoanut butter

Raw almond butter

Mix "butters" together.

Raw pecans

Raw cacao nibs

Red or white wine

Spread honey around outside rim of wine glass.

Stack Cocoanut and almond butter mixture on top of honey

Stack raw pecans on top of nut butters

Sprinkle cacao nibs on top.

Chill.

Add red or white wine.

Makes a great drink and dessert.

the Argentine center, the fabulous restauarants beckoning her to join them.

Herself in the heart

buildings, healing all those who gazed upon them. Ah, amazingly she found

From these beautiful

the energy of the Florida bay and the Atlantic ocean. Deep magic poured

Buildings drawing in

She found herself in the heart of the financial center, the huge crystal glass

And to the planet.

Miami, the global city, the gateway to the connectedness of the Americas

She was in beautiful

Sedona was amazed. It was year zero, the age of enlightenment and here

Do IT!

sharing her good fortune with others. I think I will have lunch at Buenos

Creating, writing, and

love, using the energy to bring about great miracles in her life and others,

Time, she basked in the

cosmos, pulsing through her. She felt magic, deep love, and most of the

Love energy of the

light beam in her heart. It was her connection to the divine and to the pure

Track when she felt the

heart, as she thought of her role. She always knew she was on the right

Head, through her

vibration, the love she radiated. A light beam ran through the top of her

joy by feeling her

enlightenment, here to be in love and joy so that all around her would feel

in the new age of

her paddleboard; she felt completely in her power. Sedona was a shaman

Ocean, perfect for riding

enjoyable. And combined with the clear, magical waters of the Atlantic

All the more

began to reach out to her. The rush of the wind off of Key Biscayne made it

The Latin beat

Tailored and offsetting his skin. He smiled again, his eyes enveloping her in

Formal, perfectly

Look, even though he was in a suit. The suit was black, white shirt, very

Rather romantic, exotic

With deep black hair, wavy, and long, over his collar which gave him a

Well built and athletic

When she noticed an Argentine businessman smiling at her. He was tall,

Just been seated

break from the world of international banking and finance. Sedona had

Having lunch, a

dining experience. It was filled with businessmen from the financial district

Had a wonderful

in the restaurant were an attentive staff, almost all male, ensuring everyone

And everywhere

at the restaurant, she knew it was a place of magic. The decor was beautiful

When Sedona arrived

smiled at the thought of meeting her neighbors, just a few blocks away.

Aires ANYTIME, laughing; she

vineyards and was

Did. Her beloved, Mooladara, head of an investment banking firm; owned

Was exactly what he

Away to Buenos Aires for a holiday in the Paris of South America. " Which

Will sweep you

"Ah, my lovely, I will bring us a Malbec that will make your heart sing and I

Perigon or better."

The tango with me each week, and we seal the deal with a bottle of Dom

Conditions; you dance the

He kissed her hand, every so lightly. She smiled and said, "On two

you marry me?" as

Of her table, gently took her hand, and said, "I am in love, my beauty, will

He stopped in front

Of confidence, all male, she could feel his energy as he moved toward her.

walked with an air

Been waiting for her que to approach her, he began to walk toward her. He

Say hi." As if he had

She smiled back, nodding her head just briefly as if to say, "Yes, come and

Kindness and fun.

A pristine beach near the

There was a special place on Atlantis just right for their honeymoon.

Atlantis.

part of Atlantis. Sedona was thrilled she and Mooli were stopping in

pyramids which were a vital

land and record your rememberances of the temple and the crystal

The healing of the

former glory. If you had been an Atlantian, you could visit and contribute to

restoring the island to it's

Special visas were available to the healers and historians,

Earlier in the year.

Sedona to visit her beloved Atlantis, which had risen out of the ocean floor

the gateway island, for

they married in Miami before they left, making a brief stop in Bimini,

For Argentina

which were picked at midnight on a full moon. He and Sedona left Miami

The juice of the grapes

Edge. His wines were natural, raw wines, made in such a way as to preserve

always on the leading

An expert winemaker himself. His specialty was the great boutique wines,

Name was La Dicha, the

Vortex with a 60 foot waterfall bordering the property. The waterfall's

Place, an energetic

Montana del Edyn, her Costa Rican paradise. The retreat was a special

Retreat, La Dicha in

Mooli spent a few days on Atlantis and then off to Costa Rica to visit her

Vibrant. Sedona and

The physical body of age 17 and live for hundreds of years, healthy, happy,

Enlightenment to have

Retaining their knowledge and wisdom. Yes, it was possible in the age of

Physically and yet

Back in time to a time of perfection of their bodies, each age 17, perfect

rejuvenating, the clock rolling

Sacred union amplified by the power of the vortex.

The energies of their

Vortex was known to all. Their first evening together was bliss, basking in

The immense energy of the

Their first sacred sexual union in the energies of the new continent.

Atlantis to celebrate

Place of the temple and the crystals. Sedona and Mooli had waited until

Cabanas to soak up the energy from the vortex. The main lodge housed the

Outdoor decks and

Beautiful crystal casita's were built into the side of the mountain with

The mountain,

Containment of the sacred feminine energy of the waterfall. On the side of

Created a natural safe

A circle around the waterfall, fireplace, and ceremonial area. The trees

Green, trees formed

Merging togehter in the healing space. At the base of the land, a ring of tall,

Water, air, and fire,

Water cascaded down on either side of the fireplace, the energies of the

Sat around the fire,

Fireplace was constructed, an eternal flame for love and passion. When you

15 foot free standing

Flowed down the side of the mountain. At the base of the falls, a massive

Healing. The waterfall

Recreating the energetic space she made when she began energetic

Space on the land,

Spanish word for bliss, or good fortune. Sedona had created her healing

Offerings. The winery was named "Pairings", in honor of Sedona and

Sedona's food

Winery on the property, making the freshest wines in the world to pair with

vineyards for an organic

Paradise and their visit was fruitful. They were beginning to plant the

Rica. It was truly a

World class spa at Montana del Edyn, and the vitality and energy of Costa

Mountains, the

Week, enjoying paddleboarding on the beautiful Pacific ocean, the beautiful

In Costa Rica for a

Center for the study and practice of awakening. Mooli and Sedona stayed

arts, and was a

The retreats were for corporate executives, those interested in the healing

Attending the retreat.

Enlightenment; meditate, attend seminars, and simply relax with others

Recipies of

Gathering room and pool; where the guests came to eat Sedona's special

Kitchen, the,

Beautiful life.

Yes, it was a

Raise the vibration rate of the body and regenerate the cells upon contact.

Crystals were used to

Other. They visited the famous crystal regeneration center where huge

Their love for each

Which produced some of the worlds most fabulous wines and expanded

Mooli's vineyards

Great joy in introducing Sedona to the life in Buenos Aires. They visited

Light. Mooli took

Peace and the dissolvement of fear. Buenos Aires was a beautiful city of

Of love and

Itself and it's people to a higher vibration, a beautiful time of the flowering

becoming, transforming

Country, Sedona reflected on how truly enlightened the planet was

Argentine wine

As they left Costa Rica and began the flight to Buenos Aires and their

In marriage and in business.

Mooli's partnership

End of Book Three

The

Sacred

Masculine

energy

DECENDS

They meet at the heart in unconditional LOVE

RISES

energy

Feminine

Sacred

The

revitalizing them, the unconditional love energy of the divine cosmos, strong, enduring,

streaming through their bodies. They continued to loop the orgasm through each other, their

combined energies even stronger than each of their energies alone, perfectly balanced, the

male and female energies in each of their bodies, and the exquisite balance of the male and

female energies in divine sexual union. As they began to hold each other now, still locked in an

orgasmic release, they stayed together for half an hour, the orgasm continuing to flow, to

regenerate them, and build their love for each other. The orgasm continued for both of them

for hours, a full body orgasm heightening and enlivening every cell of their body. They felt deep

love and gratitude for the divine and for each other. Their bodies so relaxed, so calm, so

peaceful, there were in an energetic zone of no stress, profound joy, and perfect healing of

their bodies, any obstacles in their bodies being dissolved in both of them. The sacred sexual

cycle complete for the moment, provided limitless energy to both of them, rejuvenating them

in total love and joy. This was the time each of them grounded the energy to each of their

bodies, loving each other, and loving themselves. As a final act, each of them created a